The Light That Heals

The Light That Heals

Keith Wrassmann

AVAILABLE LIGHT PRESS
Maineville, Ohio

Copyright © Available Light Press, 2022

All rights reserved. No part of this book may be reproduced or used in any manner without the prior written permission of the copyright owner, except for the use of brief quotations in a book review.

Printed in the United States of America.

ISBN: 979-8-9866486-2-0
ISBN: 979-8-9866486-3-7 (ebook)

Library of Congress Control Number: 2022948032

First Edition

Published by Available Light Press, Maineville, Ohio.

www.availablelightpress.com

Visit the author's website at www.keithwrassmann.com

For Nicole,
with whom I write life.

Contents

Lifeline	*15*
Distance	*16*
Find You	*17*
Breaking	*18*
Rebirth	*20*
Inheritance	*21*
You Are Not Over	*22*
Acceptance	*23*
This Is Why	*24*
You Will Heal	*26*
Flood of Light	*27*
Darkness Ends	*28*
Bitter Leaving	*29*
Unconditional	*30*
Breakthrough	*32*
Mirror	*33*
Mental Warfare	*35*
Heal	*36*
Let It Go	*37*
Reveal	*38*
You Choose	*39*
Affirmation	*40*
Birthright	*41*
Blessing	*42*

Return	*43*
Pattern	*45*
Resolution	*46*
Departures	*47*
Desire	*48*
First Flowers	*49*
Extended Light	*51*
The Hope of Living	*52*
Nature	*54*
Surrender	*55*
Live Again	*56*
Phoenix	*58*
Overcome	*59*
The Wind	*61*
The Key	*62*
Depths	*63*
Remember?	*65*
Perspective	*67*
Hope	*68*
Forward	*70*
Moving	*72*
Transmute	*73*
Persevere	*75*
Essence	*77*
Regret	*78*
Birth Light	*80*
Resolve	*82*
Hopelessness	*83*

Self-Permanence	*85*
Disarm	*86*
The Edge	*88*
Process	*90*
Present Darkness	*92*
The Way I Will Move	*93*
Floodwater	*95*
Inner Wars	*97*
What Life Was	*98*
Who You Are	*100*
Completion	*102*
Descent	*104*
Unexpected Ways	*106*
Fear's Nature	*107*
Failure	*109*
Change	*111*
Trauma's Pain	*113*
Become	*115*
Reach	*117*
White Sand	*119*
For the Sovereign	*121*
Worthy	*123*
The Light That Heals	*125*
The Gold That Stays	*128*
Thematic Subject Index	*131*

*I love you now,
and have always loved you,
and will always love you,
through your beginning,
through your ending,
until you return
from where you came.*

The Light That Heals

Lifeline

Dear Soul,
you who have descended here,
no matter how dark
or desperate your life,
always have the spark of light
available to you.
This is your lifeline.
This golden spark of light
is what you have forgotten
about yourself,
and what you can discover.
It will lead you
in and out
of all you will experience and do.
This light inside
is the part of yourself
darkness cannot hide.
When you are ready,
pierce the shadow of yourself
and waken from the dimness of the dream.
And when it is time to leave,
fear will fade away,
and the light will lead you home.
This is your destiny.

Distance

Resurrection
was not an option,
so you took the hit again
and withdrew into yourself.
It was the safest place
you could go.
And in the depth of suffering,
the time that promises
to heal all wounds
stopped ticking.
So you processed the words
you wished you had said,
and the words you wished you
never said.
And then time began again,
and you came back out
from the depth of yourself.
What was it again? you thought.
Time made it hard to remember.
Distance is a salve
that loosens the grasp of pain,
that erases grief,
like disappearing ink across the page,
like words you forgot you said.

Find You

If you have gone away,
I will come and find you.
I will not let you sit alone
in the dim moonlight.
The night does not deserve you.
If you have faltered
somewhere on the path of life,
I will remind you
that to falter is not to fail,
but to be reset to grow.
And if you are grieving
an untimely ending,
I will remind you
that there are no untimely endings,
only departures for more golden shores.
If you have gone away,
I will come and sit beside you
until you are ready to return.

Breaking

The heart longs for love
like the sunflower traces
warmth across the sky,
always desiring its light.
The pull is equal
to that of physical survival,
and does not relent with age.
When suffering the absence of love,
the heart sends warning signals
as if imbued with the knowledge
of millions of years of experience,
that this is not the way
things are supposed to go,
that this is not how life continues,
that there is something wrong
with you.
This is a lie.
The heart impresses its desires
upon the soul,
as if to guide the way of human experience.
But you are already love,
and have come from love.
You will return to love.
The experience in flesh
rips and tears at your soul.

Desire this, it demands.
Seek that. You lack.
But you do not lack.
You are already full.
You are already whole.
We break to gain the wisdom
of what it means to be broken.
This is not a reflection of a flaw
but an indicator of royalty.

Rebirth

Better times will come.
The world will change,
and you will find refreshment
for your soul.
Change brings opportunity
to reverse loss,
like when spring brings back
color to the world,
and the sense of newness
like the snowdrops
whose early bloom rejuvenates
the pale earth.
Do not fear the dim season.
Instead, find solace
in the time that builds
before the break—
the anticipation of hope restored—
like how the new day longs for the moment
the first orange sunray
pierces the dark sky.

Inheritance

We come from everlasting light,
from the golden realm of love
that glistens
like the morning sun
on untrodden grass.
All life long
we give and take,
in the hope that
our giving and taking
will fulfill our need for relationship.
Although we fall,
we are not fallen.
Although we drown,
we are not drowned.
Although we are buried,
we are not dead.
Our light burns inside,
and the harsh winds of life
can never extinguish it.

You Are Not Over

You are not over,
regardless of your loss,
your grief,
your struggle
to be and become.
You are not over,
no matter how bad it hurt
when he did it,
when she did it,
when you did it to yourself.
You are not over,
even when you thought
you could take no more,
and told yourself you wouldn't,
but you did.
You are not over,
although the thing you loved
the most
left you
like a child in the darkness.
You are not over,
because you are never over:
light is not the absence of dark,
but dark is the absence of light.

Acceptance

Once, life was this way,
now it is that way.
The change you resist
is not the new and different way,
but the process of adaptation
you now must go through
to accept it.
The heart desires familiarity.
It struggles to embrace a different path,
because now it must accept
what it has never known.
Fear is the wellspring
of unhealthy resistance.
But breathe deep.
Your heart will adjust.
In time, you will process the change
and find familiarity,
like winter, spring, summer, and fall.

This Is Why

It hurts
because it's the part of you
you were always afraid to give.
And now you grieve
because what you finally gave
was smashed to pieces
like a porcelain ballerina
dropped on a concrete floor.
But this was not accidental.
And this is not your fault.
The part of you
you were always afraid to give
is something so sacred
that its origin
is as old as your soul,
a precious gem
formed in the deep well
of your being.
Though you knew the risk
of sharing it,
you did not know the hurt.
But now you do.
And that precious gem
returns to you
as pure and beautiful

as when you offered it
in the palm of your hand.
It cannot be corrupted by rejection.
But the hurt it brought back
and gave to you
will now become your teacher.
And you will learn.
And you will recover.
And you will one day again
hold it out in the palm of your hand.

You Will Heal

You will heal.
You were made to.
You were made
to endure the hardships
that come with living.
When you are stabbed
in the back,
you will not pass from existence,
because this is impossible.
The path to life
is always open before you,
though it may be hard to see.
So, you must get up and walk.
You must take the steps
you don't think you can take.
I will live, says the soul,
*I will rise and move forward,
and nothing will hinder me.*
You must move
though you thought you were finished.
You are finished when
you say you are finished.

Flood of Light

It does not matter
where you have been,
or where you
think you are:
the overwhelming fear
that life is done,
that love is forever gone,
that you cannot recover.
These are negativities
that accumulate through introspection.
Stop dwelling on what has happened.
Stop dwelling on
where you think life went wrong.
Recognize the fear inside.
Search out its secret place,
where it hides.
It does not want to be discovered.
Shine your light on
the darkness that disrupts.
When you do,
it will have no choice but to flee.
Then lift up your eyes to see
the sun just breaking through the parting clouds.

Darkness Ends

Morning is beautiful.
It waits all night
to see you,
then when the time is right,
it gently approaches in dim splendor.
Its first light
is fragile,
like a newborn baby's first breaths,
in and out,
in and out.
And then it announces itself
like a trumpet blast.
I love you, the morning said.
You returned! the soul gasps,
I thought the darkness would never end.
The darkness always ends.

Bitter Leaving

He was supposed to leave in October,
then November and December came.
In January, I crunched frosted grass
and exhaled white wisps
all the way to his grave.
If not for the lone bird
in the barren maple tree,
I would have been alone.
The loss of those we love
is bitter,
like the sting of winter
on gloveless hands.
I am the pale, yellow sun
sinking behind leafless woods,
that has lost its strength
to warm the world.
But like the sun,
in time I will climb high again,
and you will not be able to look at me.

Unconditional

Whoever you are,
wherever you are,
I love you.
In all of your brokenness,
in all of your heartache,
in all of your pain,
I love you.
You may not understand why
the things that happen to you do,
or why
you have to fight it once again,
but I love you.
I have always loved you.
When you were born,
I watched you begin to breathe.
When you were hurt,
I watched you call for help.
When you were sad,
I watched you weep.
When you were angry,
I watched you walk away.
See, love is not a feeling,
it is a stance of conviction,
a determination never to retreat,
never to withdraw an open heart.

It is a promise that always
extends to you,
to reach you,
whoever you are,
wherever you are.

Breakthrough

This is where it stops.
Do not let fear
dictate how you feel.
Fear will run away
with your reality.
It will control
what you will do,
what you will say,
where you will go,
and what you will become.
All life long you have bowed your head
to what you cannot control.
But this is where it ends.
Infuse your heart with light
and arise gloriously.
Shout it.
Sing it.
Share it.
Fear is the opposite of love.

Mirror

I will find you
and pull you out
the other side.
You may have slipped
beyond where you thought
no one could reach you,
but I will find you.
I will look down the
darkest street,
I will search the
deepest pit,
I will walk the
barren lands,
and I will find you.
The distance you feel
between the darkness and the light
is an illusion.
Self-criticism is an anchor
you give the right to
pull you
        down to the
                depths.
But I will find you.
And when I find you,
I will take you by the hand

and cause the dawn
to shine the light of life
into your deepest sorrow,
and you will return.
You will come through.
I know this, because I am you.

Mental Warfare

Moved from here to there,
it was words that did it.
The vibrations from another's mouth
breached your defense
and set up a stronghold
in the depth of your heart.
You could not reverse it.
And now far past the realm of comprehension,
you sift your thoughts
and assess the infiltration.
The enemy will not give in.
Reason is useless.
But knowledge and experience
of past mental warfare
will lead you to
the same unopposable conclusion:
you do not believe any of it.
Words carry no inherent weight
except what they leave
upon departure.

Heal

Pull back the veil
from the seat of yourself,
and reveal your deepest wound:
a lonely child sits on a swing,
no one there to push her.
Abandonment
carries forward into adulthood.
Childhood wounds can leave the deepest,
most lasting scars on our lives.
What did I do wrong? you cry.
You did nothing wrong, the light replied,
and now, I will wrap my arms around you
and make you remember
that I have always loved you.
You are not your wound.
You are not doomed
to have the past dictate your present.
Though you may weep,
there is healing through the pain.
Though you may remember,
there is life beyond the recollection.
Though you may struggle,
hope will be your guide.
You can heal.
You can heal.
You can heal.

Let It Go

Today is a new beginning.
The night was cold and long,
but it is over.
We struggle with moving on
from past mistakes,
past loves,
past hurts and traumas.
We keep them alive
by remembering how they felt.
We think that replaying the pain
will make it go away,
or that we will understand it somehow
to make it lose its teeth.
There is no peace in perpetual processing.
Let it go.
Breathe in the cool morning air
that greets you at your doorstep.
The morning does not remember
the night,
or how it felt to wait
for the moment
the first golden hue
washed away the darkness.

Reveal

On the day of your birth,
your soul rejoiced,
though you may not remember.
Other souls delighted
as new life entered the world.
Each new life is a precious gift,
a chance for light
to enter flesh
and find its way through the world.
You are here for a purpose.
The things that hinder you
are only momentary obstacles.
The hardships of life
may mystify you
and make you forget who you are,
but this forgetting is not permanent,
it comes with living.
Eventually, you will
trace your life
back to the forgotten truth,
and your heart will rejoice.
The truth was always there,
though you could not see it.
It will show itself to you with glorious surprise,
as morning dew reveals the spider's web.

You Choose

The heart sings
based on its deepest contents:
happiness, love, joy, peace,
grief, loss, anger, sorrow.
You choose.
But I cannot choose, you say,
for my grief has overwhelmed me.
Then sing your grief.
Sing your grief
until it loses its voice,
until its inner darkness turns golden.
Do not ignore or suppress
the thing that frightens you.
But sing it
until the thing that held you in fear
is vanquished.
There is none more courageous
that one who sings.

Affirmation

Today, I will move into healing.
I will take a step
I could not take before.
I will think a thought
I could not think before.
I will throw down
whatever kept me bound
and blocked the light,
my light,
my essence,
my guidance,
my truth,
my worth.
Inner light
is a well of strength,
the spark of life.
This step today,
and then tomorrow.
Then tomorrow upon tomorrow
will bloom before me
like the petals of a rose
that unfold despite adversity.
But for today, I will move into healing.

Birthright

Hope
rose up from the ground
and took my hand.
It whispered in my ear,
Do not give up,
soon you will accomplish it.
Faith
then arose
and held my other hand.
It spoke into my soul,
I gift you with the power of change.
Love
then arose
and wrapped its arms
around me,
I have always believed in you,
and I am always with you.
I am for you, so go, and do.
And now, I will rise,
for it is my birthright,
to learn, to give,
to feel, to love,
to live.

Blessing

May peace rush over you
in the midst of anguish,
when memory
will not let go
of that which captured you,
of that which slipped through your hands,
when all you wanted
was to hold on to it.
In your distress,
may you focus not on the loss
but on the gain,
the gain that comes through the fire
of moving through the pain.
You were meant for this.
May peace rush over you
and be your guide
as you remember who you are,
from where you have come,
and to where you are going.

Return

I know you have
hidden yourself
because the embarrassment
is just too much.
No one saw it coming,
not even you.
It's the shock of such a sacred
part of yourself
splitting off,
like cutting your body in half
and watching part of it walk away.
Life brings change;
not always what we want, though.
And so, you have hidden yourself,
in the hope that being away
will lessen the burden you feel,
that you will not have to
search for words
you do not have,
or explain the reasons for
things you do not understand.
When you have been away
long enough,
and your heart has passed through
the pit of despair,

you will return.
The veil that shock pulled over your face
will lift,
and you will again
set your eyes upon the light of life.

Pattern

Walk out at night.
Go far enough and look up.
A sea of stars awaits you.
You could not see it in the daytime,
but still it was there.
This is the pattern of love.
Not the glistening beauty,
or the overwhelming sense of awe.
And not the feeling it innately pushes on you
of the questions of higher purposes
with all you have faced.
The moon attempts the same thing,
but she fails.
Too often the daylight reveals her.
But not the stars.
They disappear in the dawn,
and the world forgets they are there.
Only when the day's light
begins to fade
do our hearts return to the stars.
They wait for you
and reappear night after night
to remind you
not of beauty, truth, or purpose,
but of love.

Resolution

Where was your strength
when you needed it most,
when the unthinkable happened?
Shock stole your ability to respond.
It's the kind of shock
you don't see coming,
that bypasses all senses
and leaves you paralyzed.
It's the kind of shock
that can only come from
breach of trust.
And your heart then learned lessons
and built defenses
that pulled you from the world.
It stole your capacity
for vulnerability,
and made your soul rock hard.
With time, you saw how
the unthinkable
led to further dysfunction.
Admission is a grace that eases grief.
And now, do not let one more sun go down
before you start becoming again.

Departures

Farewell, my friend.
It is still early,
but it is time for you to go.
So I will sit alone into the morning
as the night's last crickets
fall asleep
and cease their songs.
Departures
call us into ourselves,
to journey through
the necessary undoing,
to assess the strengths or weaknesses
of the bonds of love.
But I loved, we plead,
so why does it hurt?
No greater grief exists than loss.
It is a severing
of a part of the self,
and the stronger the bond,
the greater the ache.
But even this will heal.
I will take the inward path.
I will remember you.
Though the severing,
I will be made whole again.

Desire

Do not let the success
or happiness of others
cause you to feel
insecure,
jealous,
bitter,
or unworthy.
You are not here
to compare yourself with anyone.
Human nature desires
what it does not have.
Controlled desire is healthy,
but untamed desire
overwhelms the soul.
Desire is founded on
the instinct to survive.
A cornered animal is vicious.
But you are here for
better things.
Rejoice with those
you admire.
Send love to those
who move you,
it will come back to you.
You have your own wonderful things to do.

First Flowers

Whatever your past,
it does not matter.
Somewhere, somehow,
you embraced the lie
that you cannot change
your current state of being.
You hid away the truth
that as past actions led you
to where you currently are,
future actions
will lead you
where you want to be.
This truth hides behind
the shame-barricade in your heart
that stops you from
moving forward in a healthy direction.
It paralyzes with thoughts of
you can't do this,
you don't deserve wellness,
you are not worthy of love.
But you can do this,
you do deserve wellness,
and you are worthy of love.
You are not your past.
You are your future

ever developing,
waiting to emerge
to newness from frozen ground,
like when the first flowers return in spring.

Extended Light

We struggle to love
unconditionally
because it takes putting others
above ourselves,
above our longings of
immediate fulfillment.
It requires energy that springs from
the well of completion.
It comes from a place
deep in the soul
that remembers the first light of life,
and that giving without judgment
extends this light to others.
Unconditional love
requires nothing in return.
Nothing can add to or enhance it.
To love unconditionally is difficult
in areas where we have need.
We struggle to give
what we do not have,
or what was never given to us.
But this is the pathway of growth.
Give without expectation of return.
Put others first free of criticism.
Love without first judging for worthiness.
Let love light your way.

The Hope of Living

What is the hope of living? you ask.
You are, the light replied.
But look what I have done, you say.
The light brightened and said,
I see you in the morning
before the sun has peered over the dark horizon,
when the birds have left their nests
and sing on your window sill,
when the dew highlights leaves and grass
with the silver-sparkled memory of night,
when you breathe the final breaths
of your ever-changing dreamtime slumber,
when you come up from the depths
of your innermost self
and open your eyes.
What you have done
or failed to do
is a moment that has passed
in the stream of life.
You cannot stop its flow
regardless of the words or deeds
you regret or cherish.
You have now,
the ever-present today,
to move in the newness of thought,

to rethink old patterns,
to walk an untrodden path.
You can change.
You can renew.
The life in you is capable of such things.
You are the hope of living.

Nature

We yearn toward endings
like late afternoon shadows
long toward evening.
If the journey is difficult,
the end is relief.
If the journey is pleasing,
the end is bittersweet.
Our emotions are tied
to experiences.
This is our nature.

Surrender

When you feel you have come
to the end of yourself,
and have nothing more to give
to those who only wanted to take,
there is solace in surrender.
You cannot live for someone else.
You cannot do for someone one else
what he does not want.
You long to give others
the good in you,
but one can only accept
what he has capacity to receive.
For you, surrender is not failure,
it is self-preservation,
it is allowing the greater hand
of consequence
to fulfill its role.
Sometimes it is the most
loving thing you can do.

Live Again

The pain will not last forever
but will end.
All the memories you harbor
for better or for worse
will ease in the distance of time.
This journey is not meant for
looking back,
but for moving forward
into the expanse of
what is possible.
You hurt because you loved.
To love is to hurt
because what is perfect
lacks nothing.
Love's desire is to meet
with its same perfection.
Unrequited love
is the heart's deepest wound.
Recovery is affected by
the angle and thrust of the
loss.
But you will recover.
You will heal.
The pain will not last forever.
You will move forward once again

into that expanse
where the soul is disencumbered,
where you will again feel,
again love,
again live.

Phoenix

This is for you, dear Soul,
who fell into herself
and could not find the way
back out.
This is for all the times
you held out your heart
only to pull it back
to perceived safety.
Unrequited love was not your fault,
you who loved time and time again
before turning inward.
It is time to try again.
It is time to risk it all
as if you had nothing to lose.
But you do have something to lose—
the safety that solitude brings.
But this is a loss worth losing,
as unconditional love
has a safety of its own
that surpasses that of solitude.
Flood your heart with light
until you cannot help
but rise again.
Your soul is fire.
Your future is waiting.

Overcome

When we forget who we are,
we handle life's turmoil
only from the perspective of
flesh and blood humanity.
When hardship,
struggle,
trauma,
or grief come,
they dominate and overwhelm the senses,
prompting a response
from the threat of human survival.
Defend, attack.
Run, fight.
Give in, give up.
And then later, lingering states of
anger,
depression,
hopelessness,
self-pity.
From this perspective,
the physical controls the spiritual,
capturing its light and dimming it,
dictating actions and emotions.
When our light dims
to this point of being unrecognizable,

we have forgotten the first word
that spoke us into consciousness.
We have forgotten our nature
and that the seat of the soul
is established on something greater
than what is physical.
We have forgotten that we have power
to respond to life's chaos
from the part of ourselves
that sees through this present world
and into what is eternal.
In the face of turmoil,
acknowledge the physical, but do not acquiesce,
recognize its reaction, but do not concede,
honor its response, but do not surrender.
Move from a physical-only perspective
into a spiritual point of view
that understands this experience is temporary,
and that you have grace
to overcome this world.

The Wind

Was it the wind that whispered,
You can do this,
as you stood before the mountain?
Did the wind push
and brace you from behind
as you took the first daunting steps
of ascent and discovery?
Was it the wind that cooled
your sweaty face
when exhaustion set in?
Did the wind hold you back
when you tottered on the edge?
Was it the wind that brought
a subtle chill
to comfort you in your effort?
When you have nothing left to give,
when you think you've reached your end,
when you long for a hand to help you,
I will be the wind for you.

The Key

We do not understand ourselves.
We come from golden realms
and walk the earth.
For a time,
the flesh conceals our light.
And while it is hidden away,
we strive for understanding,
for acceptance,
for love.
We lust for
money,
sex,
power,
physical beauty.
Our deep-seated desires are formed
by the need to survive.
But you know all this.
You have always known this.
When you awaken to remembrance,
your light will dawn and rise,
and break through the facade
the brief time here builds.
And then you are free.

Depths

I can't believe this,
I keep saying.
Will it ever end?
It's all I never wanted—
loss, hurt,
severing, loneliness,
anxiety, panic.
Fear weighs me down
and accumulates in my soul.
I am in the depths.
But I remember,
within the deepest despair,
hope remains.
Though the candle flickers
as darkness closes in
for the final strike,
it still has a flame.
It still has life.
Darkness has not won.
I will remember.
I will remember my innermost self,
that sacred part of me
the darkness cannot touch,
a diamond that cannot be destroyed.
I have been here before.

Was it a memory
from a dream?
Wasn't it like dawn's first light
that met my sun-parched soul?
I will find it again
and sit in the seat of myself.
I will sit in the seat of myself
and remember.
I will sit in the seat of myself
until I can see through this darkness.
I will overcome
what tried to overcome me.
I have been here before,
and I will overcome once again.

Remember?

If life has mistreated you,
it may feel like the end,
with no easy options,
no way to escape the darkness.
The human heart has the
innate ability to expand,
to love,
to feel.
It also remembers
and stores your experiences.
And trauma
inscribes its emotion on the heart
like a brander's iron,
claiming you as its own.
Trauma wants to keep you
locked under its power
to make you remember
and relive the pain.
But you are here for better things.
You do not belong to trauma.
Your heart is greater and more powerful
than anything it may experience.
Healing comes from within.
The same heart that remembers the pain
is the same heart that remembers

your beginning.
You were birthed in purity.
You were birthed in rare light.
And so, you will heal.
You must,
not merely from human will
but because of your nature.
Let your heart's light burn away
the brander's mark
by remembering who you are
as each new day dawns.
You will escape the darkness.
This is not the end.
You will heal.

Perspective

If I am lost,
it's just for now.
I know enough of being lost
that it's only temporary,
as all things are only temporary.
But as it's easy to find joy
in the good things,
it's also possible to find sorrow,
if I work at it.
Likewise, it's easy to despair
in troubled times,
but tougher to find peace,
though this is possible.
In being lost I see
that my joy or sorrow
is not truly dependent on the circumstance.
It's dependent on how I view
what life brings.
The lens through which I see the world
is curved,
and I may move it until I see clearly.
If I am lost,
it's just for now,
and it's not so bad.

Hope

May hope be a light
for the inner darkness,
when all other means
of sight have failed,
and your compass
can no longer find the way.
Hope is the wellspring of ingenuity,
the final defense
of the heart.
Hope is the most reliable
of all the soul's facets,
that when it turns
toward the darkness,
it flashes a brilliance of light.
Its nature is to strive
to find the way.
It will spur the creation
of something out of nothing.
Hope is ever seeking,
ever working,
always evolving.
It never quits,
never gives in,
and is always faithful.
Hope is your soul's safety net

when you think you have
no more options.
May hope be the ever-present light
to find your way
through inner darkness.

Forward

Today is a day of moving forward.
Yesterday is over.
Who you were
or who others thought you were
does not matter.
What you did
or what you did not do
is not what you will do today.
The power of the past
is to haunt the mindset of the present.
It robs possibility and potential,
steals joy and positive desire.
But you were born
with the power to overcome.
This is who you are.
Overcome the power of the past
by the decision to move forward.
And then move.
And then watch—
your past will transform
into learning,
wisdom,
knowledge,
and understanding.
You will remember

joy,
peace,
patience,
and purpose.
And then look—
all your hidden beauty will display
like the butterfly just breaking out of its chrysalis.

Moving

Change is difficult.
We will do almost anything to avoid
what we cannot control.
No one wants to be moved
before he is ready,
before she is willing.
And whether it's necessary
or not is irrelevant.
It's the pain.
Or the fear of pain:
the uncomfortableness,
the unwelcome newness,
the soul's forced expansion
to adapt and accept
what is unfamiliar.
The fear of an unknown future
shivers the bones,
like fall going into winter.
But change is the path of growth.
There is no growth
except for what we move
out of and into.

Transmute

You fear grief
because of the grief of the past.
The pain of loss and longing
watermarks the heart
with its signature emotion.
And now you will process
all that has happened
in the letting go.
In time, the pain will diminish,
and you will recover.
But the fear of grief
is a learned response
that hides in the shadows
of your heart.
It remains dormant until you
nudge it with thoughts of uncertainty.
The *what if?*
and the *what happens when?*
hone in on the darkness
to stir it into consciousness.
But grieving is the heart's way
of dealing with loss.
The fear of grief
is the pain of processing.
It's the pain of the remembrance

of love.
It's the *I don't want to go through this again.*
But the remembrance of love
is the balm of healing.
It's the one thing loss can never take away.
It's the bond that the severance
can never break.
It's what remains for you to cherish.
It can transmute the fear of grief
into the sacred ground of presence.
Love never truly ends.

Persevere

When you cannot find
words for the hope of living,
I will say them to you.
The world was made for you,
though you may not understand
its highest highs
or its lowest lows,
or why they both exist.
They are for you,
so you may know
the fullest range of what is possible.
Experience is the giver of understanding.
But it is difficult, you say,
I am overwhelmed.
It's when you are at the bottom
that wisdom presents itself to you,
that knowledge opens to you,
that understanding unfolds.
Difficulty brings potential for growth.
Pressure reveals truth.
Life is hard
but is worth it.
Your soul is growing
and changing in ways
you will discover.

You will recover.
You can do this.
When you cannot find
words for the hope of living,
I will tell you I love you.

Essence

We grasp to retain
and make a part of ourselves,
as if we needed anything,
as if the emptiness we feel
is determined by what we have,
or do not have.
This is fear.
We yearn to fill ourselves
with things we acquire,
as if taking from the outside
will validate our inside,
or add to it,
or make its light brighter,
or confirm its insecurities.
But this is impossible.
There is nothing outside
that can equal our essence.
You are enough.
You have always been enough
since your light first dawned.
Light can never end.
The sun never truly sets
but only appears so
from a certain perspective.
The sun does not desire more light,
because it is light.

Regret

The burning in afterthought
is too much today.
All you would have done
now looking back
is an inner fire,
and all you wish
would have gone differently
is the fuel.
The mind replays regrets
like moving pictures on a screen,
ever examining the moments
that cause alarm.
When those moments appear,
they bring with them
the sense of white-hot doom.
And anger is its easily disgruntled companion.
You burn because
you cannot change the past.
But what is done, is done.
You cannot rewrite what was written.
Do not let your light fuel
the flame of regret.
Instead,
let the courage of acceptance
extinguish all thoughts of fear

until their embers cool,
like when the last of the
fiery red sun
disappears in the depth
of the dark blue horizon.

Birth Light

Far beneath the heart's ability
to express
love,
hate,
fear,
or hurt,
the core of yourself rests immovable.
It gives rise to your
thoughts,
emotions,
desires,
and intentions.
This is your sacred ground.
This is your garden of Eden.
This is the temple of your birth light.
It is always connected to that
from which you came—
the life light of your existence.
You move through the world
as the expression of light,
and from this perspective,
what do you lack?
Nothing.
You allow yourself to experience
the swell and ebb of life,

the gain and the loss,
the pleasure and the pain,
in the promise that what remains
is the expansion of yourself.
From this perspective
you are love,
you are hope,
you are peace.
You are an endless well of life.

Resolve

When hurt, we retreat
into a deeper part of ourselves
to try to move behind the grief,
the heartache,
the pain,
or loss.
This is the soul's reaction
to the trauma life brings.
Our light recedes momentarily inward,
to reflect, to diagnose, to recover.
We put up new defenses
to thwart future potential hurt.
We make new strategies
for moving through the world.
At some point, we return
from our inwardness
and step out in front of
all we felt and experienced,
in the attempt to move beyond it.
This is our resolve.
This is our nature.
We innately strive to press forward
regardless of any obstacle,
like the bravery of childbirth
in the moment of impending new life.

Hopelessness

Fear gave birth to hopelessness
as its loneliest child.
Hopelessness sits in darkness
and refuses to let in light.
Its only offering
is to tell you of the memory
of past love, success, or victory.
Its sting is to tell you
these things
have disappeared forever,
that they will never come again.
Hopelessness
is a defense mechanism
human nature employs
to try and protect you from failure.
In its twisted intention,
it means to keep you from trying,
for failure threatens human survival.
Hopelessness
oozes false sentiments of comfort,
that life is easier
if you stay where you are.
Never believe this.
Hopelessness' blind spot is that it
underestimates your light.

It misunderstands the eternal depth
of your ever-living soul.
It can only keep you dimmed
for as long as you allow it.
Focus your light to transmute hopelessness
into hopefulness,
for you are a survivor,
and light never fails
but lives to try again,
and again,
and again.

Self-Permanence

Nothing is permanent.
The things I thought in my youth
are now foreign to my mind.
Living gets you there.
Living is a perpetual moving forward
into an ever developing present.
The present of yesterday
is not the present of today.
All things change.
The heart changes.
Desire is an undulating ebb and flow
of a soul moving through the world.
How should I proceed today? the soul ponders.
Do not blindly follow desire, the light replied,
for the desire of today
may not be that of tomorrow.
So, I will move forward
into the unchartered waters
of tomorrow's present,
knowing that when I arrive,
I will not be the same.
But on looking back,
I will find that it was not my past self I left,
but my present self more realized.

Disarm

Living without fear
does not mean living
recklessly,
but living without being controlled
by what scares you,
by what may harm you,
or by how you think you may
fail.
Fear is the most powerful
of all human emotions.
It can both save your life
and dominate it.
We remove it from its life-saving function
and misapply it to our
dreams,
desires,
intentions,
and expectations.
Fear paralyzes and burdens living.
It stops you from putting forth effort
to create new paths,
to envision new possibilities,
to move in new ways.
To live without fear
is to understand its purpose

and set its boundaries.
Permit it not to pass
into your goals and aspirations.
Should light fear darkness?
Light disarms fear.
You are in control, not fear.

The Edge

If you are struggling on the edge
deciding whether to step off,
then this, dear Soul,
is for you.
Pain pushed you
into the deepest part of yourself
where introspection dictated survival.
You sat down next to
the thing that hurt you the most
and stared into its eyes.
Why did you do this to me? you shouted.
It did not respond.
It never does.
So you fled.
And the pain grew.
By its presence,
pain's purpose is to tell you
something is wrong.
It is not the cause itself
but is the indicator
of the offense to your heart.
It ruthlessly begs you
to examine the offense that gave birth to it.
Pain will continue
until you deal with the offense that caused it.

There is no simple forgetting.
Numbing it is useless.
You have to confront it.
Return to the deepest part of yourself
and stare into the eyes
of the thing that hurt you the most:
What are you?
Examine its facets.
See it for what it is.
Clarity will come.
Understanding brings realization.
And realization is the healing and freedom
that you are not bound
by another's darkness,
nor are you forever harmed by another's actions.
Your light is powerful
and able to disarm
the things that would cause you harm.
Rejoice when you have found healing,
for the dawn awaits,
and it is time to rise.

Process

We curse the journey
because we do not accept
it is the necessary process
of moving to the destination.
In doing there is growth.
But it is impossible, you say.
What is possible is realized
one step at a time.
The hardship of starting out
will ease and give way to
the stride of perseverance.
And it is here, where the soul is tested.
In struggle, there is learning.
You can do what you set out to do.
Though the journey may cost you
grief,
disappointment,
hardship,
or frustration,
the reward is in the arrival.
And looking back from there
reveals the satisfaction of the accomplishment.
And looking ahead from there
is like stepping onto warm sand
for the first time

and staring out over
the magnificent expanse of ocean,
brushed with new possibility,
new opportunity,
new hope.

Present Darkness

The daffodil rushes
to break winter's cold,
to usher in color
to the long-dimmed world.
Its first white and yellow
mark a new beginning.
The soul rejoices, *At last!*
My hope has arrived.
The long winter is over.
It is hard to be human.
We long with all our might
for release from darkness.
When light comes and brings relief,
we then look forward with anticipation
to all we before
only struggled to imagine.
I will live again, the soul affirms.
Hope is humanity's master stroke.
It is the key for revitalization
and return from obscurity.
Hope always finds the way out.
Today, may you sing of
the coming of spring
and prepare for your impending arrival
through this present darkness.

The Way I Will Move

In the midst of this turmoil,
I will not falter.
Something better awaits.
I will not return
to the mire of negative thoughts,
emotions,
depressions,
hopelessness.
Enough of fear and its children.
When the task at hand is daunting,
fear raises its intimidating head.
But I have set its boundaries,
this much and no more.
I have more important things to do.
No time to entertain
what tries to make me believe
this is impossible,
because this is not impossible.
It is the way forward.
I will rejoice in the struggle
because hope finds the way.
I will take up a shield of faith
and extinguish doubt's flaming arrows.
This is the way I will move.
Through the struggle, I will

grow,
learn,
progress,
change.
And in this, my light will increase.
My light will expand
and surpass the universe
to gain the perspective
that sees through the darkness.
And in this way, I will arrive
and take a seat before the king
on his throne of light,
in the realm of light,
with the golden light of life between his hands.

Floodwater

Denial is human nature's dam
that stops the floodwater of acceptance.
And we rush to patch the holes
as we constantly look for weaknesses
in the barricade.
In loss,
we block the pain of permanent severance.
In hurt,
we block the uncertainty of vulnerability.
In heartbreak,
we block the embarrassment of rejection.
We cannot see beyond the present moment
because we do not want to experience
anything more.
The loss, the hurt, the heartbreak
were enough.
But breakthrough comes
when we peer over the barricade
to see what lies ahead.
Life continues.
You continue.
Let go of the mighty effort
to maintain the dam.
Cleansing and refreshment are plentiful
in the water of acceptance.

Residual pain will lessen.
No longer let fear block you
from necessary processing.
You can do this.
You can move into healing.
When you let go and accept the things
that cause such pain,
you will become like the tree
that releases its leaves
for the coming winter,
in the knowledge and solace that
in the inevitable spring
it will come to life again.

Inner Wars

It's time to move.
You have been held back long enough
by the things you could not change:
the hurt,
the grief,
the loss,
the depression,
the anxiety.
These are all inner wars
you have fought with yourself,
but now is the time to claim
what belongs to you by birth,
by your nature as a
beloved soul of light.
The physical world is dark by design,
but you have a radiance
darkness can never overcome.
Solve the trick of darkness,
and your light will radiate
brighter than a thousand suns.
This is your true self.
You have come from love.
Light is love,
and nothing can stand against you.

What Life Was

In the same way sunrise
is different from sunset,
so is our coming into
and going out of
this world.
Sunrise holds promise
for the day to come.
Its first light is a wonder
as it paints away the darkness.
It banishes all fear
and radiates
hope,
potential,
expectation,
and anticipation
of all there is to come.
The new light of life
is an unstoppable force of love.
And when the sun has run its course,
it heads toward the mysterious horizon.
It brushes the sky
with an overwhelming sense
of awe, wonder, and appreciation
of all that has been accomplished.
You are beautiful in your beginning

and in your ending.
And when the last light
has faded back into the darkness,
and you awaken as if from a dream,
you may ask, *What was life?*
The light will respond, *It was for you,*
it was of you,
it was you.

Who You Are

When you feel like the night
will not relent,
and your eyes will never again
see the light of dawn,
remember who you are.
You are above all beloved
by the one who brought you into existence.
The being of light
who made the world
in all its beauty and wonder
is the same one
who purposed you to be here
to experience it.
This means you come from
a realm of eternal light,
although you do not remember.
This means your beginning
is unfathomable
to human understanding.
In the brief moment
you walk through the world,
you explore the creator's mind,
for there is nothing that can exist
apart from it.
This too means, dear Soul,

that the night has purpose,
intrigue, mystery.
It allows opportunity
for discomfort, turmoil, pain.
In healing, we realize purpose,
growth, understanding, wisdom.
The soul lives on past the darkness.
When you feel like the night
will never end,
remember who you are.

Completion

Fear grew and alarmed you
that you would not do
all you wanted to do,
that life would end
before you got the chance
to fulfill all goals,
to achieve purpose,
to see success from hard work,
to reach others,
to live unencumbered from need,
to find requited love.
Fear noted your expectations
then exploited them.
It assessed your life
then trespassed the boundary
of your soul,
as if this were about mere physical survival.
But this is about your expectations
and the uncertainty of the impact
of unrealized desire.
What belief system
causes such an inner reaction?
Happiness and fulfillment
are not based on human accomplishment.
The soul is not threatened for survival

based on human desire.
You will do
all you are here to do.
It is written into your soul.
In the end you will see
all the pathways of your growth,
and it will not be the end
but another beginning.

Descent

You took everything so seriously
in your experience of earth.
What was it you forgot?
Was it a half-awake dream
of a faraway land
where you could not tell the difference
between reality and illusion?
And illusion
became your reality.
It can do that.
Life can do that.
And then suddenly
you straddled the edge of this world
and the next,
wanting to make a fearful escape
but not knowing where to or how.
I love you.
I promised I would
before your dream took hold
and you plunged into experience.
Life is experience.
You dreamed of and longed for
the world
from the perspective of
invincibility.

But to live
is to be vulnerable.
If only our human eyes
could see past the edge
of flesh and blood
and remember the golden light.

Unexpected Ways

In the depth of despair,
I will hold your hand.
I will comfort you
with sunlight and shadow,
coolness and warmth,
hunger and fullness.
I will speak the language of your soul,
though you may not perceive it.
I will inspire new dreams
and weave them into your future.
I will create paths for you to walk
before you take any steps.
I will sing a healing song to you
as you drift off to sleep.
And in your dreams,
I will show myself to you
in unexpected ways
that though unknowing, you will know.
All this I will do, dear Soul,
to remind you I love you,
and have always loved you,
and will always love you.

Fear's Nature

When I understood fear's tactic
of imposing radical alarm on my soul
at any opportunity,
I asked it why.
*Because it's my job to alert you
to potential harm,* it said.
Thank you.
You may do that
when my life is in danger,
but you may not do that
when I am striving for growth.
You may get my attention
if I am facing a physical threat,
but you may not do so
when I am planning future endeavors.
You are forbidden to act on hypothetical scenarios,
or overreact due to past experiences.
And you are absolutely prohibited
from acting on any uncertainty
I may have of forward movement,
as I will learn and adjust as appropriate.
Struggling,
failing,
learning,
and growing

are mine to do,
not yours to deter.
I do not need you to
cast doubt on my dreams,
which is your greatest character flaw.
You may no longer run wild
but must stay within your bounds.
When I understood the nature of fear,
fear fled,
and creativity, faith, and hope
took back their proper place.

Failure

The fear in failure
is that you are not good enough,
that you are inadequate,
that you cannot fulfill your purpose.
And you feel
shame,
embarrassment,
humiliation,
dissatisfaction.
You may even curse life,
or stop trying.
But what if failure
was a necessary part
of an imperfect world?
What if failure
was a master teacher
who showed you exactly
where and why you went wrong?
Do not be discouraged.
Failure grants wisdom
to those who will listen.
Failure is the great encourager
who gives you the ability
to try again
with the advantage of hindsight.

Failure is an endless well
of insight.
Its pain is momentary
and will give way to perseverance.
Remove fear
and you will be free to fail.

Change

Today, I will grow.
I will face the challenge
I avoided in the past.
For too long, I have let fear
dictate my willingness to engage.
But not today, not this day.
There is too much ground to gain
for where I am going,
and fear is not allowed to follow.
I envision change
and can feel its presence,
like the coolness of fall
when summer ends.
Something is different.
As I strive to newness
and leave the old way behind,
I will not lament the time spent there,
for it has passed like all time, with
good,
bad,
positive,
and negative.
I will accept the past
as part of the process of growth.
And I will welcome the struggle

to once again be remade,
to continue the journey of becoming,
of discovering,
with gratitude for this
opportunity of living.

Trauma's Pain

Trauma has a lasting pain
that does not easily let go,
and is only noticed
after all has been said and done.
Trauma's pain is triggered
by certain
words
places
thoughts
feelings.
The mind stalwartly monitors current experiences
in the fear of repeated hurt.
This is the mind's attempt
to protect you.
When it recognizes similarity,
it warns you with a flush of memory.
This is trauma's pain.
It makes you relive
the hurt of the moment,
over and over,
until it no longer knows the threat.
Trauma's wound is deep.
But you can heal.
Convince your mind
that the threat is gone.

Remember who you are.
Remember from where you have come,
and where you are going.
Do not deny the original pain
of the original wound,
but accept that it has spoken
and told you what it needed to.
And then dismiss it,
as it has done its job.
And you survived,
because you are a survivor.
The light inside you
knows the way to healing.
It knows how to cast away the darkness
like when winter breaks,
and the earth is new again.

Become

No longer say *yesterday*.
Only passing moments exist,
some of joy,
some of sorrow.
We mark time by the minute,
instead of by the experience.
In doing so, we thicken the veil
that we are time's subjects,
enslaved to its beginning
and its end.
You do not belong to time.
And do not say *tomorrow*,
for you have not arrived there,
and the expectation to become
may steal your joy from the now,
or enslave you as the master of your dreams.
But say *today*,
for this is where you always are.
Yesterday and tomorrow
are illusions we envision
in judgment of our being,
our process of becoming,
our movement of growth,
our regrets and wishes,
and our achievements.

But live today,
for this is your yesterday and tomorrow.
You are constantly moving and becoming.
For today, become.

Reach

How does the heart recover
after such a loss?
You were shipwrecked
in the wake of grief,
and on your way
down to the depths.
Reach out your hand.
There is help in the ask.
There is hope in humility.
Human nature does not like
to need anything.
We think we should have
all the answers.
But this is resistance
to the light of others.
Reach out your hand.
There is love.
Someone will help.
The light of another
can reach you in the darkness
and pull you back to yourself—
this is the common bond
of one soul to another.
We are from light
and are of light,

and recognize ourselves in others,
that if one is dim,
the other can brighten him.
Allow the grace of light.
This is the way we heal.

White Sand

The soul's link of consciousness
to the human body
rests above all human
emotion,
desire,
pain,
and fear.
We take up residence here
the same way we leave upon death
and return from where we have come—
as a white wisp of wind.
The soul gathers experience
like the farmer gathers the fall harvest.
We benefit from a world of
good and bad,
right and wrong,
pleasure and pain,
joy and grief,
health and sickness,
happiness and sadness.
Fairness is not part of the equation.
We curse the bad
even though it is the necessary counterpart
to understanding what is good.
This is the design of the world.

You are here to rise and fall
with the tide of life,
to know the fullness of
what it means to live.
But you are not here to drown,
as this is impossible,
for drowning would mean you end,
and you do not end.
Regardless of how and when you leave,
you are greater than when you arrived,
and have done what you were here to do.
And you will continue,
to be,
to become,
to stand on the edge of the everlasting shore
and feel the warm water forever
wash away white sand between your feet.

For the Sovereign

The descent into flesh
requires forgetting who you are,
for a while.
You must move as if you have never known
what it to means to live,
without hindsight of the golden shore.
And though your origin is royalty,
you will become like all others
who glimpse true beauty only in a dream.
The struggle of human nature
is its base physicality,
its overwhelming instinct to survive.
It will cause you
to do,
to feel,
to think,
to respond,
to desire,
to fear
in ways that seek to preserve its life.
You will be so profoundly enmeshed in flesh
that you will think this is your true self.
You must overcome this.
The world does not remember its light.
This is by design.

But you, dear Sovereign,
are the light of the world.
It is you who have come
to conquer the darkness,
to be the guide for those who cannot see.
And your light will overcome,
and others will see your deeds
and hear your words,
and you will leave a legacy of how to move,
of how to live,
of how to love.
And when the time comes
for your light to fade,
a multitude will greet you at the golden shore,
and welcome you to golden realms of light.
Then you will remember in full,
and the light will heal all pain,
and wipe away your tears of memory.
And you will sit upon a golden throne
with a crown of glory resting on your head.

Worthy

All your life
you have looked outside yourself
for what would fill you,
what would satisfy you,
to be found worthy,
to be made whole.
All this longing was an open wound,
a mark on the soul that birth left.
Though the forgetting is in the descent,
the memory of completion
remains in the secret part of you,
because it is you.
Human nature drives desires
of social connection
and outside approval.
But self-worth does not come from others
or exterior impulse.
You are worthy because of who you are,
not because of what you do
or what others think.
Upon waking to remembrance,
you can move past the human fear
to fit in,
to be good enough,
that you need to earn love,

that you need to prove yourself.
It is an illusion imposed at birth
that what
is
by its nature
needs exterior confirmation of its existence.
You are enough.
You are whole.
You are complete.
You always were
and always will be.

The Light That Heals

When I close my eyes,
I see it far off in the distance.
I sense its goodness,
though I cannot reach it.
I almost remember it,
but I cannot place it.
It comes closer.
Golden streams of light
shimmer and dance
as they pass through the door of
my invisible eyes.
The light grows brighter.
And all my sorrows,
all my failures,
all my regrets
are exposed in its radiance.
My future as well
is revealed in the light.
What are you? my soul requests.
Am I you? Are you me?
It does not answer.
Instead, it pulls me forward.
I am afraid.
I am before the light.
My invisible eyes are obliterated

in its presence.
My senses begin to close,
and all I know in this moment
is that I exist,
alone
but not alone.
I am one
with myself,
with the world,
with all who have come before me,
and all who come after.
The light is love.
I no longer fear.
I now remember
when time began,
when I first became aware
of my own beginning.
And the light said,
I love you now,
and have always loved you,
and will always love you,
through your beginning,
through your ending,
until you return
from where you came.
The light pulls away
and recedes.
My senses return.
My invisible eyes see

the pinprick of light
that still shimmers
far off in the distance.
I weep,
for I know the path I must take
to return to completion.
And all my failures
are not failures,
all my sorrows
are not sorrows,
all my regrets
are not regrets.
They are life,
nothing more
and nothing less,
life
in the light that heals.

The Gold That Stays

I know death
feels like permanent loss,
a forever separation of relationship—
to call for and not hear from,
to look for and not see,
to lose the safety and benefit of love.
Be it so, from the human perspective.
But though you can't perceive the golden realm,
its existence is a truth
even your forgetting can't erase.
To you, here and now,
its truth feels like a lie,
because everything here fades.
You see this in the flowers,
in the leaves,
in yourself,
and as dawn gives way to the day.
The illusion is convincing.
But this is the nature of
this present creation.
Death is the necessary counterpart
of a temporary world
for passing out of this life.
But it is not the end.
You never end.

You know this in the deepness of your soul.
In death, you let another go
but only for the moment feel the pain,
as in time you too will go
and take the passage opened once again
that leads you to the golden realm of light,
to reunite with those you told goodbye,
to share forever what you learned of life.
This is the gold that stays.

Thematic Subject Index

The poems in this book contain a variety of themes. Sometimes, a single poem will touch on multiple themes. The following subject index lists out some of the more major themes and highlights where they are more prominently featured.

Birth: 38, 80, 123

Death: 29, 47, 99, 128

Discouragement: 55, 63

Encouragement: 20, 21, 22, 33, 42, 61, 92, 106, 109

Fear: 23, 24, 27, 32, 72, 77, 83, 86, 102, 107

Grief: 16, 17, 39, 73, 82

Growth: 72, 90, 93, 103, 111

Healing: 16, 26, 36, 40, 56, 65, 88, 95, 117

Hope: 20, 28, 41, 52, 68, 75, 92

Human Nature: 18, 23, 48, 54, 59, 62, 65, 78, 82, 83, 95, 102, 107, 113, 117, 119, 121, 123

The light speaking: 36, 52, 85, 98, 125

Loss: 29, 47, 73, 117, 128

Love: 30, 41, 45, 51, 106, 125

Origins: 15, 21, 59, 62, 65, 77, 80, 97, 100, 104, 117, 121, 123, 125, 128

Purpose of life: 15, 38, 41, 75, 80, 99, 102, 119, 125, 128

Recovery: 16, 26, 29, 40, 49, 52, 56, 58, 63, 70

Suicidal thoughts: 88, 104

Trauma: 24, 35, 36, 37, 43, 46, 65, 82, 113

About the Author

Keith Wrassmann holds the degrees of MA in Creative Writing: Poetry from Miami University (Oxford, OH) and MDiv in Theology from Cincinnati Christian University, where he also won the Theological Studies Award. He has served as a shepherd and teacher in the church, enjoys screenwriting, and writes the blog www.theologia.blog. He lives in the greater Cincinnati, Ohio area with his wife and children.

Visit www.keithwrassmann.com for more.

Made in the USA
Coppell, TX
16 December 2022